T0395562

What Happens Next?
DEALING WITH LIFE CHANGES

What Happens When
I Have ADHD?

Emiliya King

PowerKiDS press

Published in 2026 by The Rosen Publishing Group, Inc.
2544 Clinton Street, Buffalo, NY 14224

Copyright © 2026 by The Rosen Publishing Group, Inc.

First Edition

All rights reserved. No part of this book may be reproduced in any form without permission in writing from the publisher, except by a reviewer.

Editor: Caitie McAneney
Book Design: Leslie Taylor

Photo Credits: Cover GUNDAM_Ai/Shutterstock.com; p. 5 Studio Romantic/Shutterstock.com; p. 7 DimaBerlin/Shutterstock.com; p. 9 Andrew Angelov/Shutterstock.com; pp. 11, 15 fizkes/Shutterstock.com; p. 13 Miljan Zivkovic/Shutterstock.com; p. 17 oneinchpunch/Shutterstock.com; p. 19 pics five/Shutterstock.com; p. 21 A.RICARDO/Shutterstock.com.

Cataloging-in-Publication Data
Names: King, Emiliya.
Title: What happens when I have ADHD? / Emiliya King.
Description: Buffalo, NY : PowerKids Press, 2026. | Series: What happens next? dealing with life changes| Includes glossary and index.
Identifiers: ISBN 9781499452457 (pbk.) | ISBN 9781499452464 (library bound) | ISBN 9781499452471 (ebook)
Subjects: LCSH: Children with attention-deficit hyperactivity disorder–Juvenile literature. | Children with attention-deficit hyperactivity disorder–Education–Juvenile literature. | Attention-deficit hyperactivity disorder–Juvenile literature.
Classification: LCC RJ506.H9 K46 2026 | DDC 618.92'8589–dc23

Manufactured in the United States of America

Some of the images in this book illustrate individuals who are models. The depictions do not imply actual situations or events.

CPSIA Compliance Information: Batch #CSPK26. For Further Information contact Rosen Publishing at 1-800-237-9932.

CONTENTS

Paying Attention

Imagine you're in class. Your teacher calls on you and asks you to repeat what she just said. But you can't. You weren't listening. You were looking at a bird outside the window. It was **distracting**! "Paying attention" is very hard.

This might happen to anyone from time to time. However, for people with ADHD, this inability to **focus** happens all the time. They may also feel **frustrated** or restless. If you have trouble paying attention, it's not your fault!

Your Point of View

ADHD stands for "attention deficit hyperactivity disorder." More than 11 percent of kids in the United States have been **diagnosed** with ADHD.

More than 7 million U.S. kids have ADHD. You're not alone if you think you have it!

What Is ADHD?

ADHD is a condition in which attention and self-control are difficult. Kids may seem **disorganized**, careless, or even rude. They may make careless mistakes on their schoolwork or need to be reminded to finish tasks.

Kids with ADHD may also be hyperactive, or unable to sit still. Being patient or waiting to do something might seem impossible. Sometimes they may do something they know isn't the right thing, like talking in class. That's a sign of poor **impulse control**, and it's common with ADHD.

School can be hard for kids with ADHD. It may look like they don't care about rules or grades, even if they do.

Your Point of View

People with ADHD may fidget a lot—or make little movements over and over—when they're feeling worried, bored, or trying to pay attention. This may look like tapping feet or fingers.

Getting Tested

If you have trouble in school, you can tell your parents or caregivers about it. Describe how it feels when you struggle to pay attention or sit still. Your teachers may even talk to your parents about it.

Your parents or caregivers can take you to a doctor. They may send you to a special doctor—one who deals with ADHD cases often. They will ask you questions about your attention and impulse-control struggles. It's important to be honest about how it affects your daily life.

Your Point of View

Psychologists and psychiatrists are doctors who work with mental health conditions. Some of them focus on ADHD.

When you tell your doctor about how you've been struggling, they can come up with a plan to help you.

Dealing with the Diagnosis

You might feel unhappy with a diagnosis of ADHD. You might feel weird about having that "label." It might make you feel different from the other kids around you. Those feelings are normal and okay.

You can also look at your diagnosis as a win. There's a reason why you have been getting in trouble or struggling to learn. Now that you have a diagnosis, you can find out how to make it better. Your parents or caregivers will probably tell your teachers and get the right supports for you in school.

Learning you have ADHD might be a relief because now it makes sense why you struggle when other kids find things easy.

Your Point of View

People with ADHD sometimes call themselves "neurodivergent," which means their brains work differently from the "average" brain.

Extra Help

Once you have a diagnosis, you can get the extra help you need for your ADHD. Your parents or caregivers can learn how to help you stay organized and on task at home. They can be patient with you and give you just one task or piece of information at a time.

Teachers and support staff at school can help too. They can help you stay organized in school. They can give you breaks to move. They can break up your work into smaller pieces.

Your Point of View

If your parents want you to clean your room, they might help you by breaking it down: "First, make your bed." That will make it easier to complete the task!

If you're distracted looking out the window in school, the teacher may move your seat closer to the center of the room.

13

Therapy and Medicine

Some kids with ADHD go to **therapy**. This is where they can talk about what they are struggling with. Their therapist can tell them how they can deal with their hard feelings. They'll also give them tools for greater impulse control.

Certain medicines may help kids struggling with ADHD. They can help you pay attention. They can allow your brain to slow down enough to take in information. Not all kids need medicine for their ADHD, but it can really help those who do need it.

It might take a little while to figure out what works for you: therapy, medicine, or both. In time, you'll find the right fit!

Your Point of View

Always listen to your doctor's instructions about when and how to take your medicine.

Your Support System

Many people can support you as you deal with your ADHD. It's important to have a strong support system, or people who are there for you when you need them. You may need extra help, but you may also just need to talk.

Your parents, teachers, doctors, and therapists can give you the tools you need to succeed. Friends and family are also important. Find friends who accept you just the way you are. Explain to them what ADHD is and let them know when you're struggling.

You can also join support groups for kids with ADHD. This can show you that you're not alone!

Your Point of View

There is no **shame** in having ADHD. You can be honest with your friends. If they are good friends, they will be kind and helpful.

17

Things That Help

It may not seem fair that things are harder for you than for other people. But you can grow your skills and use tools to deal with everyday situations. At home, you can have your parents or caregivers help you organize your room. Remove any clutter or distractions. Keep a calendar to remember when things are happening.

At school, you can sit in the front and center of the class. Make to-do lists to stay on track. Learn to **prioritize** your assignments. When are they due? What will take longer?

Your Point of View

Keep a routine, doing the same things at the same time each day of each week.

Exercise can really help boost your attention. You can try running, swimming, or doing sports like basketball.

19

You Can Do It!

You can do anything that your peers can do. You might need extra help or tools, but you can achieve anything you set your mind to. Look to famous people who have dealt with ADHD, such as Olympic athletes Simone Biles and Michael Phelps.

With the right support and an attitude of **perseverance**, you can learn in school. You can succeed in sports, art, or music too. The most important thing is to never give up.

Your Point of View

Some people with ADHD find **white noise** or fidget toys helpful for paying attention. Find what works for you!

Simone Biles struggled to sit still in school. This made learning hard, but it also helped her train as a gymnast!

Glossary

diagnose: To identify a disease by its signs and symptoms.

disorganized: Unable to keep things clean and ordered.

distracting: Drawing away attention.

focus: To direct attention.

frustrated: Feeling angered or let down.

impulse control: The ability to keep oneself from acting right away on urges.

perseverance: The quality that allows someone to continue to do something even though it's hard.

prioritize: To list or rate (as in projects or goals) in order of importance.

shame: A painful feeling that someone has done something wrong or is wrong in some way.

therapy: A way of dealing with problems that makes people's bodies and minds feel better.

white noise: Constant background noise.

For More Information

Books

Bernstein, Samantha. *ADHD Is My Superpower*. New York, NY: Windmill Books, 2023.

Holmes, Kirsty. *ADHD*. Buffalo, NY: Kid Haven Publishing, 2025.

Websites

ADHD
kidshealth.org/en/kids/adhdkid.html
Read more about ADHD with KidsHealth.

This Is Simone
www.timeforkids.com/g56/this-is-simone-biles/
Explore the story of Simone Biles, an Olympic gymnast who lives with ADHD.

Publisher's note to educators and parents: Our editors have carefully reviewed these websites to ensure that they are suitable for students. Many websites change frequently, however, and we cannot guarantee that a site's future contents will continue to meet our high standards of quality and educational value. Be advised that students should be closely supervised whenever they access the internet.

Index